Pull-Out Poster Book

SCHOLASTIC INC.

New York   Toronto   London   Auckland

ISBN 0-590-06663-3

™ & ® & © 1997 by Lucasfilm Ltd. All rights reserved.
Published by Scholastic Inc.

12 11 10 9 8 7 6 5 4 3 2 1   7 8 9/9 0 1 2/0

Designed by Joan Ferrigno

Printed in the U.S.A.   08

First Scholastic printing, February 1997

C-3PO and R2-D2 approach the palace of Jabba the Hutt — beware!

"You underestimate the power of the dark side."

C-3PO under the watch of a Gamorrean guard.

Sy Snootles and the Max Rebo Band play alien music.

The carbonized Han Solo — Jabba the Hutt's favorite decoration.

Jabba the Hutt holds Princess Leia captive — but not for long. . . .

The galactic bounty hunter Boba Fett battles with Luke Skywalker.

Luke Skywalker in the fight of his life!

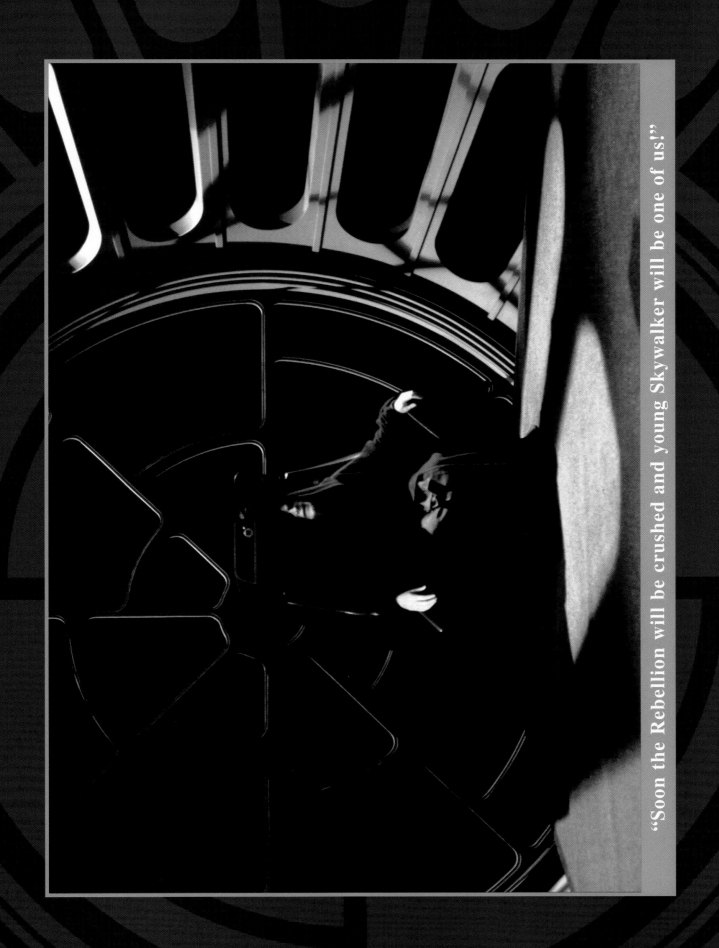

"Soon the Rebellion will be crushed and young Skywalker will be one of us!"

This Imperial scout trooper is out of commission.

One-meter-tall Wicket the Ewok.

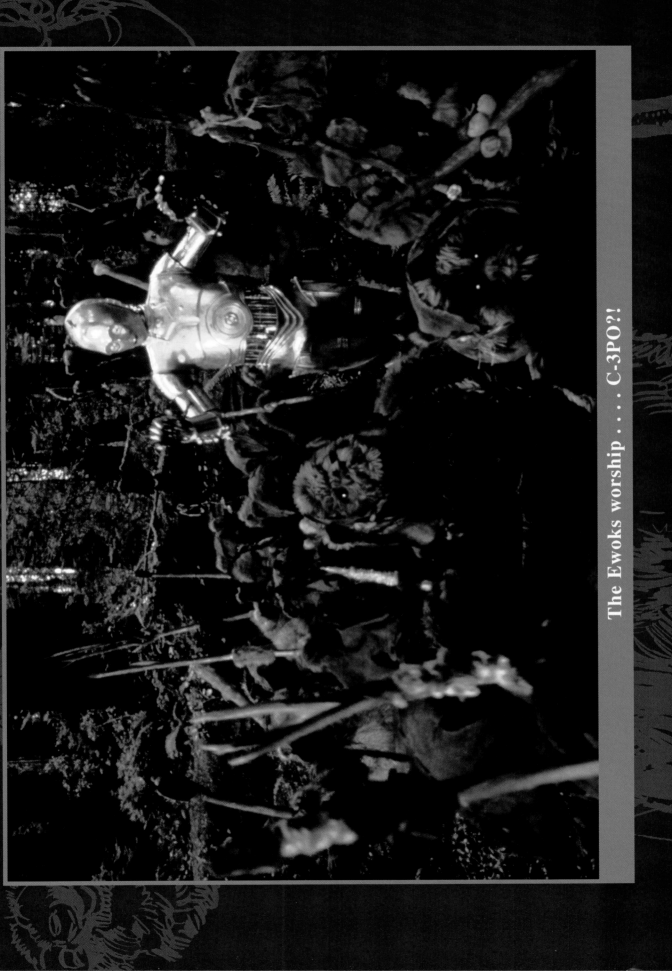

The Ewoks worship . . . . C-3PO?!

Han Solo storms the shield generator bunker.

Luke Skywalker battles Darth Vader — and the dark side of the Force.

Lando Calrissian and his copilot, Nien Nunb, prepare to destroy the new Death Star.